Vampire Burrito
FIRST EDITION

Copyright 2023 Matt Mitchell
All Rights Reserved
ISBN 978-1-7353527-8-7

BOOK DESIGN BY KEVIN LATIMER, CASTER IMPRINT
Garmond, FangSong, Adobe Pro, Cochrin

COVER DESIGN BY MATT MITCHELL

this book is published by
GRIEVELAND
grieveland(dot)com

"O minutehand, teach me / how to hold a man the way thirst / holds water. Let every river envy our mouths. Let every kiss hit the body / like a season. Where apples thunder / the earth with red hooves. & I am your son."
—Ocean Vuong, *A Little Closer to the Edge*

"Have a bunch of kids who'll call me Pa / That must be what it's all about."
—Bob Dylan, *Sign on the Window*

"And shall, what with all the interest / I bear toward plans of yours and the future / Of stars it makes me thirsty / Just to go down on my knees looking / In the sawdust for joy"
—John Ashbery, *Riddle Me*

"O beautiful / was the werewolf / in his evil forest. / We took him / to the carnival / and he started / crying / when he saw the Ferris wheel. / Electric / green and red tears / flowed down / his furry cheeks. / He looked / like a boat / out on the dark / water."
—Richard Brautigan, *A Boat*

THIS IS A BOOK

ABOUT BEING INTERSEX
ABOUT BEING INFERTILE
AND ABOUT BEING IN LOVE

VAMPIRE

BURRITO

DRACULA'S THEME

VAMPIRE OF THE NORTH COAST

Few things terrify me quite like the skitter of unholy hands
        across a keyboard in the guts of a home I'll never enter.
What is living proof to a king uninterested in the way a DNA clusters?
            Has my vulnerability not been up to par?
Have I not unhinged my jaw far enough into the laps of those playing god?
Peel back my cock and you will find 25 years of womanhood beneath it.
      I shouldn't have to say anything more.
On National Intersex Day, I find myself no longer enticed by the exit of light.
I am far more in love with how it breaks through a prism of glass.
        and turns someone's face into a bullet of pale like mine.
I am much more content being a dog barking
at the bottom of a pool, or an erasure poem unpublishable.
To combat 46XX with a shotgun of hormones is like a weekly suicide
        without the grief.
When the two-headed calf saw twice as many stars,
            was it not the beauty we spoke of first?
When I wake up and find myself flirting with the pulse of two sexes,
     it is the legibility of their beats that is questioned by murderous fingers.
You cannot be two things at once without first being desirable enough
to a blade unwilling to end you.
No one has ever said *He is intersex, so I want to fuck him*. But maybe someday they will,
and maybe that is why I am celebrating my body on a Tuesday morning.
But to wish yourself a Happy National Intersex Day,
        you must first get catcalled as a faker by someone like you
who disagrees with how undedicated you are to a life of pain.
They've got me dead to rights, I tell you. A friend says I look tired.
It is because I have once again become the dust of Adam
        caught in a vacuum of community that doesn't want me
to celebrate this dick or these testosterone injectors
or the habitat of womanly proteins in the nucleus of my every living cell.
      I am all bone like a windchime!
But someday I will proudly spool my lips around an afternoon
of warm clothes and bottomless hormone cocktails,
amongst a stomach of unsure eyes. One day I will not enter
my name into the search bar of an app built to destroy me.

My body will no longer bend to the body that came before it.
I will toddle in my own juxtaposition and so on and so on and so on.
I have long lived in a gap of nothingness, so forgive me if I am eager
to become a cycle.
The Colossus of my yesteryear has fallen;
        I am no longer interested in being instructed on how to hurt.
I am not a spokesman or an activist so much as I am pillaged
by a circumstance I have fallen madly in love with.
Like Richard once said: "The dead will make room for me."

                      Sadly, it's the living I'm not so sure of.

GRAY AND GOLD

after Frank O'Hara, Richard Siken, and John Rogers Cox

Turned brittle from the UV lights
of an airplane cabin,
I thought about whether or not anyone
picked Lana Turner up after she collapsed.
Enveloped by walls of bodies repurposed into metal;
Tunnel vision from rows of cue ball ginger ales,
a flight attendant cut her thumb on a lime rind
enroute to Cleveland. There it was,
the plum of the world balancing
on a freight harbor and midge eggs.
Though Hollywood was mine, it became a bygone.
I'd left that body and looked forward to the snow.
I recognized the wheat fields and the cow pastures
as if they'd never turned into skylines. Gas wasn't an arm
and a leg here yet and smelled of Papaw's coveralls.
Home sweet home, the land of
A Nightmare on Elm Street and the Cedar Bog Monster.
In an airport, you can personify
the "tell me how all this, and love too, will ruin us" line
because your betrothed, disheveled and jetlagged,
tumbling through kiosk after kiosk,
as if they are swimming through the wreckage
of some great, expensive beyond,
is never going to the same place as you.
It's Shakespearean, or at least that's what I believed
it to be, once, when I was in the mood
to be inconvenienced. When I was in a comfortable love
with an uncomfortable someone.
But then out of nowhere, there she was,
dressed in moon trousers and a mustard hoodie,
awaiting her suitcase at the baggage carousel.
A genius, she used her tippy-toes to catch the forthcomings.
Love at first sight was all that and a bag of chips.
The bees knees before the replacement surgery.
In her hand, a one-way ticket to Ohio.

Beneath her chin, a neckline of gems.
I said I'd work on myself but maybe that meant
falling in love with the mirror again.
Fate does what it wants. I should know,
as the tiny pocket of testosterone in my thigh fat
has finally dispersed for the week
and didn't tip off the TSA agent.
The clamp was loosening its grip on my heart.
My therapist had mentioned something
about the patterns we can't seem to shake,
but I'd forgotten it then, or maybe it was much longer ago.
Oh Matthew, we love you, please get up!
What's the worst that could happen?
You were the starting quarterback
about to win the big game.
She was a werewolf drinking Diet Coke
under the neon of a good hair day.

FLEX

A mountain range in my jeans, I have lived through two dozen cocks
and am still unsatisfied.
       This funhouse mirror body fucks in lowercase letters
and has become real, real thin.
I don't want to be a father but I also don't want the inability to become one.
       How emo, to be chromosomally unable to play a part
in the swelling catastrophe of a population boom.
How goth, my genius can't outrun the silence of a fertility doctor
when I ask if there was ever even a chance.

THE IDES OF MARCH

I have never written about shooting
a gun before,

because the closest I have been to
an exploding barrel was when my father

taught my mother how to shoot
in our backyard years ago.

My uncle drank a 5th of angel dust
on his parents' patio in 1985

and shot himself in the head
with a twelve-gauge.

My father still hears gunshots at night
when he is asleep.

He has never read any of my poems.

My other uncle goes to West Virginia
every November to hunt

and bring back dead things for his wall.

Every March 15th, my father takes
his brother's portrait off the mantle

and stands in the same spot where
he died. He slides his feet over

the recarpeted floors, says *This could
be a poem*, and knows he'd never read it.

CHROMOSOMAL CLIT

I almost threw myself off the edge of Point Arena in front of all my friends,
because in a doorway at the end of *The Searchers*,
a hollowed John Wayne is banished from his home
        but called a hero in retrospect.
Because every six months, a blood test strokes my pussy
        and I become wet with malpractice.
It's Wednesday night, and a bulb of testosterone emerges
        from the hole in my thigh that a needle just punctured.
It's alright, I say, I can't find the clit either. But wherever you are, I hope you come home soon.
Who was it that said TO COME OUT IS TO REMEMBER HOW JOY FEELS,
  because the truth is, here I am. And the truth is I have never felt so alone.

LIZARD BRAIN

how embarrassing of you / to have so many goddamn mouths /

each one full / of unclaimed paper receipts /

spilling out of their grocery store self-checkout dispensers

aimlessly / matthew david / you sweetheart / are you telling me

you can't possibly spell goodness without god /

you act like intersex folk are the titanic / and not the iceberg /

it pains me to tell you / it is quintessentially the opposite /

nobody's gonna read a book / about missing chromosomes /

hello it's 2022 / and we're craving stories that're complete /

how do you not know how to swallow pills / how do you not

know how to swim / how do you not know how to be anything /

but unemployed / can't you call yourself something / other

than smoke in a swollen throat / just because your mother

is anaphylactic / doesn't mean you are, too / go back to therapy /

get a job / eat more fiber / i will not call you *intersex* / because

queer book award categories do not recognize it / it doesn't roll

off the tongue like *busted* does / matthew david /

you're not gonna win the pulitzer / you're never gonna be best in show /

you're never gonna win miss america / you are barely a person /

quit trying to be anything more /

how can you liken that gut to stained glass / you will never be that

beautiful / stop reaching for the light / you will never be tall enough /

how can you be so mad / when you should be grateful / we don't

call you a dickless fat fuck anymore / it took you four years /

to get a writing degree / just so you could bitch and moan /

about your chromosomes / your book is all lies and fabrications /

it doesn't have to be like this / quit victimizing yourself / you're just soft /

you know while you were trying to be a "neon" "hollywood"

"cowboy" / the bad men were erasing your brothers and sisters /

look i love you / and i'm proud of all that you've accomplished /

but matthew david i swear / if the garden of eden fell

right into your lap / you'd probably fuck around and wound it

THERE'S A ROOM WHERE THE LIGHT WON'T FIND YOU

My dead uncle was once a brown-eyed boy
who dreamt of being an astronaut in bell-bottoms,

chopping lines of angel dust on a motorcycle seat
after his second marriage fell through.

But first, a hitchhiker at sixteen
screaming up the road near Clemtown,

where a stray tornado tilted the sky's gray
onwards into pink. He smoked his teeth brown

near a hatch of frozen prairie falling
into the Tygart River dam, where Charlie drowned.

My dead uncle played a golden telecaster
that left behind thrushes of Marlboro red skeletons

in the mulched December West Virginia snow.
Fuck you for leaving me with all of this,

my dad says of him in 2017, as he quietly cares
for their dying father alone. Dad, a spark

of Copenhagen breath who'd never hit a woman,
was a Miller Lite brain acidic from a shot-up house

and a bullet put through a temple sharing same DNA
on the Ides of March in 1985.

My dead uncle almost killed Mamaw with a ricochet;
almost killed dad just the same.

A murder of bikers once wrote FUCK YOU,
MR. AND MRS. MITCHELL

in the back of a funeral guest book;
now we only speak of curated, undeadly memories

before our bruises swell into a room
and rush into a ziplocked mouth.

We always speak of how Dad broke his hand
in a mountain bike accident;

We never talk about how Papaw
had to identify the mangled remains of his eldest son.

One of the brothers busted papaw's stereo with a hammer
and then a belt broke each of their asses raw,

but everyone's lent a pass to the alcoholism on a gravel throat,
to the hush-hush and the repressed grief.

I drew a picture of my history teacher naked
like Burt Reynolds in *Cosmo* and dad pinned me to the ground,

put all of his weight into me, and said I'd end up dead
like his brother if I didn't shape up.

It was the only touch we ever shared.
Was I actually a bad seed growing romantically fatalistic

in a junior high wind, or just an unfortunate reminder
of his inability to make a more complete offspring.

A three-hour drive home and, again, Dad says he missed me,
and that his bloodline will die with me

if I don't bring another body into this world.
So much desire to grow a baby inside me, it's no wonder

these chromosomes hum womanhood.
My hand unspools into a clapboard house;

a birthright of its own trauma, sewn up and gushing
through lumped throats and turned around picture frames.

We're all afraid of death after someone else's makes us alone.
Whenever I was suspended at school, I fluffed my breasts up

in the mirror of my bedroom, in hopes of staying upright.
I am a good mother but I am an even better infertile little spitfuck,

never taught how to love generously or how to love at all.
Only how to ball a fist at a slurring death threat.

Only to be filled with the delusion that Brutus' knife
went so deep but didn't come out the other side.

TIDEWATER RAISING

A tattoo artist inks a stigmata River Gorge Bridge beneath my armpit, but he doesn't quite capture the diphthong coming from Papaw's mouth, the way he signaled he was pulling over beneath the south end to take a piss before driving us home. Doesn't capture the distraction of downstream water becoming the Ohio River, or how my thing got stuck in the zipper and I missed real bad and was covered in it. That when Papaw saw the crying and the mess and had to carry me back to the car, he put plastic bags on the backseat, buckled me in, and said *Shoot a bullet at Ohio from West Virginia and it'll never hit a damn thing either, buddy.*

STATE BIRD

America, I gave you all until I was nothing but love bug dysplasia and paper
moons laminated with recycling plant plastic. That was my inheritance,
    a birth of buzzwords transplanted
              in my mouth. Mothman, pepperoni rolls, rhododendron, ancestry.
The Camaro winding along the Devil's Elbow
          on log cabin field trips. Backseat Coca-Cola spills
                    leaving a stain that could've sent me straight to god.
The late summers spent listening to Elvis and orbiting the moon, when
the YouTube app
    was Homer's brown television odyssey. When a promise was a spit-shake
and a take-back was an ear canal full of rocks.
              Not even tweezers could be taught to pull love from that sky.
Croissants stuffed with five cheeses and pork globes gave us wings
so we could run 3v3s against the Morgantown kids
          at the family reunion and float down the court
                    in our all-black Starburys and calf-
        hugging shorts.
It was all rhinestones and tie-dye over yonder. It was playing Cowboys and
Indians in the pitch black of Aunt Carolyn's basement with cap guns and
small yells. Before Michael, I'd sit in her laundry room that had no end,
at a desktop computer with boot-up internet, and email Mom about
 the supermarket cowboy resplendent singing Slim Whitman near
            the Union Cemetery.
About Papaw drying his handkerchiefs on a clothesline above sparrow
carcasses.
              I typed about how Michael
        and I cardinal'd ourselves into the back patio door
just to become stained glass. It took her reply 30 minutes to find me,
while I was running to catch the shadow Michael left in the air
as he walked home through five backyards because
            I couldn't imagine a world, or an email, without him in it.

INTERSEX BOY WATCHES EPISODE 179 OF *FRIENDS* FOR THE FIRST TIME

Of course there is a Brad Pitt sex dream
somewhere in all of us, but at what cost?
     A GQ Sexiest Man Alive glare that can cut butter,
 like a scalpel against a trespassing cock.
What is language if not primetime punishment for those it was stolen from?
I, too, am sometimes an unfortunate product of the nineties.
A miscarriage and a birth simultaneous and ugly.
   I am a walking *Is Pepsi okay?*
A Thanksgiving turkey born undercooked despite some miraculous burning.
    I am both Ross and Rachel,
but I'd be anybody's hushed gossip
if it meant being anything to them at all.
   There are no rumors about me,
only most-anticipated-list books and learned boyness
  still abandoned on the pages nominated.
My people have been dying with every 8:30 NBC time slot
on Thursday nights since '94.
    If you're an interviewer afraid of landmines,
don't you dare say the word *intersex* without looking us in the eye.
  We have more names to give than backs.
When this chest balloons into tits,
there is no laugh track to shrink it down.
     All the hermaphrodite jokes end up on television
  because they aren't money enough for Hollywood.
  So who will make me more man than punchline?
You see, I am merely a loaded gun shooting blanks.

BACK WHEN WE HAD NOTHING EXCEPT OUR HANDS, WHICH GLOWED BEAUTIFULLY AND DREW PICTURES OF GODS DOING SOMERSAULTS WITH THE WIND, BUT ALSO SOMETIMES INTERLOCK WITH SOMEONE ELSE'S RIGHT BEFORE THEIR LEGS BOARD AN INTERCONTINENTAL FLIGHT THEY MIGHT NOT RETURN FROM

Beyond the cowboys flushed in acid,
galloping through the hotel parking lot, yodeling at snakes,

        there's a turritopsis dohrnii in California waters.
        Locals call it immortal jellyfish because it reverts

to a polyp when it's stressed or sick or old.
To live inside of a reset forever, we'd only be so lucky.

        I hope I can achieve the same endless do-over
        and wrap my arms around your body

once I stop being an iceberg and migrate back
to the coast we left behind.

        Yesterday I sang into the canyons
        and all that echoed back was wind.

A 76ers game on the television set in our living room.
They are up by 5 on the Raptors.

        Superstar Hall of Famer Absolute Godhead NBA Center
        Wilt Chamberlain slept with 20,000 women,

And if you laid all of their bodies out across the Pacific Ocean,
you would have to do it over 130 times before you could reach Europe.

                Behind paper thin walls, a neighboring room
                is watching *Seinfeld*. We were born the spring

before the summer it ended,
the summer everyone gathered in Times Square

                                to watch that show about nothing.
                                    This is a poem about nothing.

But it's also a poem about everything.
The number one song in America

                      was I Don't Wanna Miss a Thing because we all knew
                          there was so much armageddon left to see.

My cab comes by and asks where to.
I say take me to the ocean so I can fall into it

                    and coo about how Amsterdam has already started eroding
                        away into the shape of an Ohio we can't remember.

There is a dolphin in Italian waters.
America is selling out.

                    I have forgotten how to fill up a heart with familiarity.
                      But, if by some chance Cormac was right,

and you have my whole heart and you always did,
please, let those tides bring you home to me,

                              so we can relearn how to spell warmth.

So we can cut up the rug in our best chambray plumes,

dance, and glug Diet Coke like whackos.
AirBnB ourselves a heaven on Prospect,

                                      dirty the sheets, and never leave,
                                            O, so help me god.

WHITE NOISE

In a different version, I take it all back.
This five-mile-wide town becomes the size of Chicago.
                      Hoover Pond turns into Lake Michigan
in our backyard after a heavy rain, glaciers migrating and bursting and
glowing beneath Canadian lighthouses.
My dad fishes for yellow perch; I dance through puddles.
At night I tear pages from my copy of DeLillo and fold them into paper
cranes.
I hang each bird from my ceiling before kissing forbidden country bodies,
hesitant not to mistake any navels for pressure points.
                    I build homes on the sunken marshlands
of Midwestern hips while *I've thought about us for a long long time* swallows
the bedroom. But in this version, I am the same age my mother was
        when she graduated college and my farts now smell
like my dead papaw's used to. And the lexicon of this town, once soft-
rock ballads crawling from the throats of Camaro Z28s, is now an old
friend screaming "hermaphrodite fag"
        at me behind a skyline of clenched teeth.
And you can't dance to the sound of a familiar mouth betraying you.

BUILDING A BIRD

7 score and 16 years ago, the Monongahela water and cave-deep holler
    gospel siphoned my folks' folks' folks' folks' folks home from France.
Great-great-great-Grandpa and Grandma pooled their electrons together
to forge a shoebox cabin out of apple butter, Cynthia branches, and
hayseed glue. They coughed up shotguns and Civil War gunpowder and
    cicada membrane, stored coal rocks in their throats until their chest
viced them into diamonds.
When the banks threatened to flood their land,
the 13 siblings lobotomized the mines together and stole all the canaries
They hid them with the railroad bonds behind Elihue's portrait.
    I remember I never cared much for loving Papaw's granddaddy's cabin.
I remember loving all of it so much. The fish tuned for plucking,
the banjos tossed back into the lake bluffs. The hills washed bone-dry
    by well-water infections and gold-capped-toof nursing home elegies.
The shagbark hickories now eat up the mountain majesties, a white-
brested nuthatch lands in Papaw's back porch feeder and takes two extra
    portions when the phone rings.
The neighbor dogs siren a burlesque of doe stalking beyond the creek
full of burning leaves, back near whatever highway bypass they crossed
to find us.
    A phone falls to the garage floor.
Papaw says *They're bulldozing my family's cabin just for the land*.
    Not even a shopping mall, not even a housing development, not
even a mouth.
Just a gap in the muck where men were born when the sun wrapped
around them.
The next day, Papaw goes to the garage and builds a canary
out of Cynthia and hayseed and hides it in the pink insulation hollow
behind Elihue's portrait on the patio.
He comes back every morning to tend the woodburner and check for
cave-ins.

LOOKING FOR MOTHMAN

cosmically flirtatious, I too am sometimes so elusive my own kind forgets me

a similarly bodied vestibule of *I believe* bumper stickers, but *believe* in what

the aluminum bug with tits in Point Pleasant's square or just the idea of it

the pussy in my chromosomes the cock in my poems or just the talk of it

how its spectacularity is so foreign but equally exquisite

worth a thousand glances and its own museum in somewhere nowhere

everyone talks about the tits when there's a photo-op brimming

all the x-rays, polaroids, and selfie gray matter thick as AndroGel

thumb over the lens, *get a look at its wings* and *can you retake that* propaganda

yes, I suppose Mothman could be real

real as all of us, just a bunch of no good nobodies always grasping at light

BACK WHEN WE HAD NOTHING EXCEPT OUR HANDS, WHICH GLOWED BEAUTIFULLY AND DREW PICTURES OF GODS DOING SOMERSAULTS WITH THE WIND, AND THE HEARTS OF MILLIONS SAW OUR PICTURE IN THE PAPER AND WISHED US LUCK

Love of my life dancing in a wedding dress the color of rainbow trout,
    we cooked ourselves from clotheslines and pigeon-pecks on a Sunday,
when young men ran suicides and hugged themselves into brain damage a mile north.
    Our vows talked against atoms of a sky not yet rotten with shouting.
        We pinky-sweared a forever.
            Holy matrimony is learning how to worship something
    that isn't silk-screened on a T-shirt,
or: recognizing the grooves worn into my steering wheel as yours.
It takes 4.3 years for the light of the Alpha Centauri star to reach us.
With that kind of time you could build 226 new Earths.
        I wonder how many of those Earths I would live on,
        how many times I could kiss you,
again, for the first time, in a parking garage, and remember to hold onto it.
    I'm as tall as Terminal Tower, you said, once we reached the top.
        We just got married! we told the harbor.
    When the world ends, language will swallow all of the light.
    Our only lanterns will be these poems. The birds are calling us home!
        For so long I believed I was the dragon.
    But when I met you, I realized I am the princess.
You said *Take me on a date*, so I broke up with the sun and fell in love with you.
When I couldn't understand how astronomers know so much
        about the sun, how they can predict the life of something
they can't touch, you said to think of the Clevelanders falling to their knees
    at the sight of the Cuyahoga River burning, whispering,

How beautiful this warmth. How impossible to put this all back together.

AU REVOIR

A pair of lips holding a curious mouth skids around the stretch mark beside my right breast and stops. Not to admire the entrance of change but to compose the interest's exit music. A hiking trail sutured shut. A flashback to a high school lover sucking on my tits like they were her own, then followed by an asking of if my cock could reach, would I titty-fuck myself. Looking in the mirror, pushing my gazongas together. Rubbing them up and down. Stretching them apart until they ached. Wearing the back brace as high as it'd go. No tight tops. No white shirts in the pool. Those cans were not serpents, but oceans. All natural and heavenly undiscovered. Yet there is still a forced shame about land not yet called beautiful. Despite the chesticles of junior high, sans bean dips and nurples, my nipples have always been supple. Pink spheres composed of smaller, more delicate spheres. Salmon goosebumps. Dime-sized areolas still likened to pepperoni not by reality but by principle. But with one flick of an index still comes a telescope of hardness, no matter the size. With one lip swirl comes the same. Now at 25, thin wands of hair like a skirt around the pinkening, as if an avalanche protecting Everest's teeth. Montgomery glands rid of oil then stuffed with lavender. A testosterone level of 300 or less will forever maintain a B-cup. What was once a locker room interrogating my tig ol bitties is now a garden asking where the soil went. This is not like the hipbone predicament of 2015. No cousin to the blades around my waist shrinking in a precious darkness of puberty. No, this was an eradication of the best part of me. The jugs that once reached, briefly, beautifully, and slowly, toward the ground, grasping for sea level. You two, globed handfuls of salt, how could you pull me into the earth and then so proudly leave?

PRUNTYTOWN, WEST VIRGINIA

The industrial home for boys was a mile or so out of the way from our route
    to the Dairy Queen,
        but we drove past it intentionally,
to memorialize my electric dinner tantrum in a seafoam Dolphins jersey
        Mamaw bought me from the back of a JCPenney book.
My tongue of cobbed corn: sponged, fissured, and vulgar.
I learned it from Papaw, how to say curse words longer than my arm.
And those mashed potatoes and steamed carrots *did* taste like shit.
But all of that fuss boiled into a promised puberty of bread, water, and a cot
as punishment.
The momentary threat of family abandonment and the removal of every
window.
                How will the birds find me?
      I ate the M&M blizzard without making a mess so I could wake up
in the warmth of tomorrow.
        The industrial home closed 15 years before I grew from my own
father's rib.
Yet I still remove my own just to bend over backwards for him and the rest
who share our name.
And that name, it means *Gift of God* in whatever language isn't this one.
One day my stomach lining will torch itself into a shrinking skyline,
and I will still have to make sure it doesn't leave a stain in whatever shadow
decides to stick around.

CITY OF LIGHT, CITY OF MAGIC

Everyone's favorite celebrities keep dying but you are still here, therefore
I am okay.
What could be more us than a Tuesday evening,
    as we climb back on the wagon and take lawn chairs downtown
to watch the skyscrapers get built after a lifetime of standing
on top of ourselves for a view. You've wreaked havoc on the world
      yet your hands are unequivocally perfect to me
       despite the incapabilities of my stupid own—
when every hidden inch of me will soon be a bruise,
and whatever I am only exists when renewed
          on Wednesday nights, by a tip of pinprick
     touching exhausted fat, under glow of living room light,
as I reintroduce my fingers to my thighs weekly.
Yes we look like fools, making eye contact with widowers. But I need you
close, as my concave chest somehow shines beneath a streetlight
until you put my head under your hoodie and there's nothing but snow.
    You say your biggest dream is to find someone
      to search for D.B. Cooper's treasure with.
I no longer tell anyone they're the most perfect person in the world
    because it is a lie, because so often you lend me your closeness,
so often you hold me until I have again remembered
    how to discover an above prickled with airplanes.
Werewolf I was made to love you, and someday we'll depart each other,
But first I pull a deathbed from a pothole and toss it back,
      kissing away its ridiculous and curved familiarity.
      These seats we brought are reserved for the living.
   I need you close, close enough to at least gently pull
the pads of your fingers across the goosebumps on my wrists.
    Close enough to hear the last note sung by a sharp thing falling
from 200 feet above our kissing, uncontrollably laughing heads.

WE HAD AN APARTMENT IN THE CITY

Late evening, back on Detroit Avenue again, we sang in grief and heart-eyed
ourselves beneath bedazzled street arches. The college kids threw spirals of
animatronic vomit down the sidewalk,
        drank in a ballgame by the Happy Dog.
I remember you there, with your white platform boots and adorable shit grin;
        I remember the way Beloved sounded a lot like your name
then, what with the syllables, the quickness.
I'd give anything to go back and slow down. Because I haven't seen you since
May, now that I've gone to live for a short while in the country,
   where dandelions grow out of tree stumps and I tell my father I love him
with a handshake.
At night the toads hurdle bumps in the driveway tar,
        we compare moons over facetime, the stars arrange themselves
                brightly into you, and I am broken glass

CHINATOWN

I think my good friend Debbie said *Don't be afraid to let your body die.*
    This was before my head squared into a Zenith television set but after dad's 3-channel manifesto and the NBA game of the week on Sundays.
        Then it was the 404 error, the corrupted gonadal spectrum, passed on through blood and learned aggression
            Sega dysgenesis, couth with one-use hospital gowns.
                Before every cell inside me up and died
the syringe told me *Forget about it Jake, it's Chinatown.*
Forget about it Jake, it's just hormone bloat and withdrawal.
            But look what it's done to my throat: the appling,
the spark of deepness, and thickening underchin.
The needle once broke beautifully in thigh fat, when the jarflies drowned in the snow. Now I have to pick up the prescription on time before the nausea hits. I've been rearranged into something so fragile I
        lose my feathers when someone else holds me too long.

IPHONE NOTES

i cannot sleep until i listen to
radio ga ga by queen 23 times in a row.
Yes, absolutely, the world is going to end.
Why?
bc there's a whole part of maryland
named chevy chase
and no part of maryland
named gilda radner.
bc the aluminum shortage killed vanilla coke.
and bc there is no god, hehe.
if there was a god,
we'd still have the seattle supersonics.
me at four years old, thinking
i made all the puddles go extinct
by stomping through them.
me at four years old, mistaking
drought for *death*.
aunt carolyn once dated a guy
who played pro ball for cleveland.
maybe they were just friends,
but in my mind they loved each other.
she sat at his bedside when he was sick.
when will they run out
of phone numbers?
my bucket list is nothing
but visiting that place in america
where you can touch 4 states at once.
uncle ben's death in *ozark*
hollowed me into an exit sign,
but i blamed it on this town.
i hope the world does end,
because, then, when this is over,
We're all going to have to answer
to the coca-cola company.
because i'd sit alone
and watch your light.

404 ERROR

we are most like animals not when we argue
but afterwards, during the faintest pull of quiet
our apartment chooses to spare,
when the autumn of lamplight breaks against our eyes,
and there's a wet on our cheeks we call oxygen
in the same way early settlers came to shore
and saw bison and called them buffalo
400 years later we call the bison buffalo
      and the buffalo extinct

from the California zebra escaping the Hearst property
to the Pennsylvania carrier pigeon picketing the mail,
they will only say you are gone
once they mistake you for living
      on your own terms

it takes my face 8 years to partially cover itself in hair,
I don't want to imagine what my heart is incapable of
but when Joey says
there are 7 other people in this world who look just like me,
I ask *did god forget to add the ovaries to them, too*
with my all of my chest

CONSPIRACY THEORIES

    Del Sol Kung Fu and Yoga became a bird sanctuary before
the pandemic. Everyone has forgotten about ornithology now because
there are no more birds. Just microchipped government drones
and AI robot nuclear warhead Terminator 2: Judgment Day bees.
      I have never been stung by a real bee, knock on wood.
      No cankered rodeo of a swollen body
  turning jelly red under YMCA pool chlorine.
I almost drowned there. Can you imagine if grime-tiled tidal waves
had been the death of all men.
We'd only be so lucky,to have all hedonistic swelts of Fortnite rage
  eradicated before ever earning a beginning.
There was a time when Del Sol was still Kung Fu and Yoga.
A time before Reddit went nuclear and killed the stonks.
      Back when I didn't miss the got damn bluebonnets.
I love you, I text you, before you jet off to a landlocked Netherlands
  from Cleveland-Hopkins. I started loving you
     long before my prefrontal cortex was fully developed,
after I stopped wearing cigarette hats and grew petrified of smoking.
Long before we solved the Cleveland Torso Murders, which felt
really out of the blue and unlike us, because it had already been a cold
case for 70 years, and we were never all that good
  at taking care of cold things,
especially our bodies in winter, when the apartment heater would kick
off before dawn.
Wednesday night before you caught your plane, you put your hand into
the hole of my thigh, where the lip of a needle once gripped, and pulled
out a dove.
You asked, *Is this your card?* Yes, I replied. Truthfully, I expected you
to pull out nothing except maybe a fruit or some pearling atoms, but
there you were,
  surprising me, like always. The only doves now are emojis.

Heart the band is now more Google-searched than heart the organ. After quarantine, there will be parades in honor of maskless skinny dipping rendezvous and kissing lovers
on their beautiful foreheads. As is customary, whenever it arrives.
    Our app-store birth charts will feel alive, when we are Halloween c-section suns,
    stimulus check moons, Adam Sandler movie marathons rising. And of course I will go to the parade, because I am obsessed with celebrations dedicated
    to things that have gone but will return.
Let's become birds one day, you text me after flirting with a common kingfisher in Amsterdam,
    so the FBI agent reading our conversation remembers it.

THE DAY OF THE EXPANDING MAN IN REVERSE

        Atoms dust the bed sheets as we collapse into each other.
Deacon Blues pours through the Amazon Echo like wildfire while a
microwavable dinner rusts in my gut. Teevee static inches down my foot
and cans of pop half-gone with tinfoil spread across the lid
        sweat on the second fridge shelf.
          You, in a bucket cap by a manmade lake at dusk,
    knock on my sternum to see if it sings. No pat hand.
Chicken soup for the intersex soul, or: stretch marks like line breaks.
Hearts strung up like Xmas lights, luck bringing a thousand years
        of paper cranes.
Growing pains in the cookie jar and skylines shaped like cleavage.
When a butterfly becomes a ballet of light, the sunburn peels reveal cub
scout badges:
fire making, first shave, stomach holes, popped tent in a wilderness of
new hair, ignored nausea.
          A back splitting in half.
Lady hips and champagne legs. Inject, wince, wipe, bandage. When I nap
I hear angels and they pin a medal on me. In an examination room, your
hand on my back as I tell the neurologist shocking my electrons that my
body's had enough.

NUCLEAR SATURDAYS

      Seems that all the Mountaineers, save for Papaw's grandad,
pilgrimaged to the Ozarks and turned the corn Presbyterian,
leaving truckfulls of coal behind for a sun's mouth unopened.
      My ancestors traded the mountains for a 1/3rd success rate,
taught us to chisel our kids from the cliffs and call them so.
Sometime between Papaw's dad's 12 brothers and sisters
and my only childness secretly cutting up the rug
with a contraband of Playboys and Hustlers
beneath a heap of blankets, came a plague of infertility in inheritance.
Was it in the summer of the town's bicentennial,
in a bluet of 1 am, when Papaw and I slung ourselves
around the house corner, and he shot the hide off a raccoon
thieving by the dumpster, and bullet shrapnel
knocked the wind thru the guts of his mercury light,
and we had to use his dentures as a lantern just to get back to the house?
A punishment for deadening the habitat just to reclaim territory,
as if everywhere I was looking wasn't already a lack thereof.
How I lost our children before calling them twinkles in our eyes,
I still don't understand.
      Overpopulation feels like a myth when you can't contribute to it.
      I'm sorry it isn't cheaper to pass down the family name.
      If I could live everything over again, I'd wear looser underwear
      and search the ends of the earth for my Y-chromosome.
      Just so we can one day tell the neighbors to lose our number,
and we can one day get to a paradise not yet corrupted by almost.

NEIL YOUNG GAVE THAT SPEECH FROM THE MOON

When we sat in the back of Dorothy's astro van and watched the buffalo
fall into potholes along I-68, we sucked on Dum Dums
from the bank and played five-finger-fillet on a history textbook.
We smelled like what was left of our dads:
baths of Drakkar Noir, suicidal ideation, and diabetes
slick like a turtleback on Juicy Fruit breath.
We each called shotgun and accidentally touched hands
beneath the fold-down cupholder. The powers that be
pushed a goldfinch inside the radiator valve.
Good grief, he sniffed out the fruit of me, when I was nothing
but a thousand suns blown out of a hot-wired chest.
After Dorothy taught me how to pump gas at the Exxon station,
she drove us to a run of water named after my great great grandad
and let us play rock-skip while she divorced her husband
over the phone. Instead, we swallowed chainsaws and choked on the air
she breathed, as the super wolf blood moon ate us both up real good.
I walked with him into the stomach of a sewer tunnel attached
to a blood-bloated prairie and then walked out stinking rotten of bone-
dry lips and dropped zippers, leaving behind a casket
of fresh smoke eating the pearl of an asshole clean out.
I faked a bee sting just to get out of saying goodbye properly.
Then, back at Aunt Carolyn's, during the grace before dinner,
Mamaw unwrapped me an unmarked butterscotch candy
slowly, afraid I'd make far too much noise with my hands.

HALF OF ME IS OCEAN, HALF OF ME IS SKY

                              Ask me if the sky is as big today
                              as it was the last time we spoke,

when I jogged along the brim of Edgewater Park
hunting for a bloating gam of whales
to photograph for us
and dry heaved from withdrawal.

                              When our eyes and our mouths
                              always took notes for the poems
                                    we hadn't written yet.

Our throne, abdicated in the name of love,
or at least what a doctor convinced us was so.

                              Even after all those needling years,
                              I am still tenderly pulled apart
                              by the celluloid bloat of a face
                              turned miserably aglow with hormones.

Scammed, by the falsehood of medicinal reward.
In high school I wanted anything but a stomach

                              full of prescription disquiet. Just one cock
                              unexamined by labcoat strangers
                              and sperm born from my own cells.

Now in adulthood I only want to write poems
dedicated to Keith Charles
saying *No matter how we get a child, we'll both win*
to David Fisher on Six Feet Under,

                              because, given my own inconclusive
                              fertility calculator and my swimmers
                              like butterfly teacups, I say

let's let those who glow just glow
and hope to someday make fire all the same.
There's a belly somewhere
now a living room painted by lamplight.

                        And if a set of intestines like tungsten,
                        then a set of breasts mistaking the sky
                        for the floor to match.

What gender is testosterone if not birdsong
singing *Your sperm's in the gutter,*
your love's in the sink
against the gonadal potency of his own winded flute.

                        Yes, I am thick as a brick,
                        in that I can't peel backwards
                        and let the garden of suns spill from my ribs.

Yes, a decadence of light, as if everything I touch
knows how to breathe except myself.

                        I know you still sleep somewhere
                        between the lips you pressed against my cheek
                        in an apartment bedroom, tonguing the sunset,
                        patiently waiting for the wind.

Our running legs the color of sunburnt lemonade
have never stopped since we met.

                        I've been told the seven saddest words in the English
                        language are "He was going to be an acrobat,"
                        followed by "You need to see a fertility specialist."

Though, it is my humblest opinion that
all sentences I speak have already been cooked.
I could be the seventh son of the seventh son.

Everything I ever am will still require an incubator.

                    So perhaps I don't have it in me to love so hard.
                        or perhaps I have never really loved anyone
                                quite as much as I have loved you.

O, to be swimming and swimming
until we cross paths again.
To never stop circling each other once we do.

SUBMISSION FEES

      I am a series of odds, a percentage for and against getting
           crushed by a fast food sign,
              a wound of garbage filled with syringes, magnesium
vitamins, and swallowed light.
      Tell me what kind of bones match my pronouns or I'll forget to
           breathe in the bath.
I was born into the vice grip of one identity and now thrust into another.
    We have been tasked with procreating something more definitive
than ourselves, with willing a glacier into a boat like some kind of god
or spork. To be miraculous is not about having the best of luck.
To be miraculous is about having enough wealth to buy the fortune.
And you know what they say about money and poetry. But I fold
         the cranes. I blow the eyelashes. I pull the bigger half of the chicken
wishbone.
If we buy an embryo the warranty expires immediately.
              A cold front arrives on the day of our appointment.
I see my nipples through my shirt and turn into a drill bit.
Perhaps this is the only time I'll ever be a good screw.
The windows are shrinking but the stained glass is still beautiful.
         You are the sunset, the pollen dusting our geraniums,
with your hair done up like the prom. And I am your windchime.
I can feel the memory of our newborn cooing in the next room.
        The examination table feels brand new,
    the scales, the blood pressure pumps, and the stethoscopes untouched.
                  These procedures must be out of season.
You kiss me and say, *This is our year*. I clench your hand within mine.
         Lamborghini started as a tractor company. Perhaps we, too,
                     have more left to give.

OPERATOR [THAT'S NOT THE WAY IT FEELS]

By noon, the town's dry heat melted summer.
On the driveway of asphalt and gravel, weeds grew beneath
a rusted black dumpster, railroad ties split the earth like dying bark.
Papaw and his brother drank Coors Banquet from the garage fridge in
secret.
Talked town gossip over a cooing air conditioner. Croce on the stereo,
John Deere tractors, mostly in parts, lined up like soldiers,
      green as Coke glass. I snuck in through the side door;
        peeled paint fell like snow onto the shoulders of my hoodie.
I hid behind a table saw and listened to them talk wild
              and spittoon tobacco.
Watched them uncoil themselves with words sharp like
pussy, motherfucker, and *goddamnit.*
Words like knives in my mouth. As the sun turned into a burning
      purple electric of garage mercury light trespass, the dark went
crooked and Papaw's brother flooded the air with questions.
                      Why I always played pretend inside
      instead of studying how Papaw got his hands grease dirty
      and all of that out here. Why those hands of
mine were so small, so ladylike. When the garage turned into a holler,
Papaw showed his brother the toolbox I used.
          Pink insulation and mountain mouths
poked through the walls, accents suspended themselves in
the dust Papaw wiped from the toolbox's lid into a ventilated breeze
ripe with oil stink when his brother wasn't looking.

PRETTY IN PINK

Nothing but a sunset shaved, I hope we get lucky by coincidence.
What was invented first, the wheel or the reusable razor?
Artificial insemination or the improbability of its success?
If you could be a glacier would you glow slowly or just be cool?
Teeth grind or continental divide? River or Keanu? Maybe both.
Binary stars, Diet Coke prodigies, silly bandz, and HitClips.
Goodness, I just think of you and can see that magic in your eyes.
For you there'll be no long wait times. No overdraft penalties.
And when you're good and ready, the world will bend to your smile.
Don't let your occhiolism show. You aren't a city quite yet!
Everything is all wild in the cleome brush,
and they carved your mitochondrial genome off a mountain
to become an embryo grown in a petri dish under a Mexican sun.
Please stay golden, even through chance.
My smol dracula, I know I am being alarmist.
But if you leave, don't leave now.
You are already my whole menacing, hopeful, electric heart.

I WILL LOVE YOU TOMORROW AS MUCH AS I LOVE YOU TODAY

The disco ball above a Starbucks wrapped itself in Christmas lights while we were away. When we returned, our bodies, lovingly, looked like apricots splayed out across the chapped asphalt, as we watched downtown fall into itself.
You said *How could I have forgotten this*,
        as if you were somehow again sitting on the couch in your mother's house, petting cats and listening to the insects eat up the night beyond a window that was, for so long, always yours.

JOHN CARPENTER'S *HALLOWEEN*, 1978

my DNA used to code me as a girl
but now I'm a hermaphrodite to virgin ears

there's a cold hand measuring my breasts
and marking the shrinkage,

saying my holster can be so strong
it floats a revolver

with the help of a weekly needle,
in the same accent Bruce says

I walked a thousand miles just to slip this skin
but has not yet left his seat

so what can be agreed on about XX chromosomes
but their sameness, their ruling class of estrogen

in a country of boy smirk,
textbook absence and all that corkscrewed goneness,

a script for testosterone becomes a subtle way of saying
This will surely kill the girl raging inside of you

thousands of kids are surgically given new names
at birth every year by men who were once students

sewn to the promise of using scalpels to fix malfunctions
upon entry, because junior year in California

someone in pre-med saw my autoinjectors
buoying through the zipper of my backpack

and said *Whatever they are will never work*
with the knife of his mouth

so now what can be agreed on about XX chromosomes
but their abnormality in a boy body

and their side effects: a fragile wind of designated sex
beating against fluid wet bone

lady-like hands beholden to a lifetime of gossip
as if to say: any of this could, and surely will, destroy you

and someday I will have to explain to my kid
that the blood of a shapeless army

has long been on the hands
of the men who pulled us out of our mothers

and announced our gender to the heavens only to erase it,
because before becoming what we always thought we were,

a doctor first looked upon us infidels—
bottles of hope shaped like handguns,

wide-eyed and crying
and not yet curled inwards away from laughter—

and decided to selfishly kill
what we didn't even know was there to begin with

I WAS BREATHLESS UPON EVERY MOUNTAIN JUST TO LOOK FOR YOUR LIGHT

Before bed, I put your pearls on the shelf, inside a Pyrex bowl, next
to the chapstick and state quarters. Rolled on your side, you ask,
Which mouth will carry us into the morning this time?
while muted Netflix glows into our ceiling, and we dream
              of the old world, where god used USPS 2-day priority
shipping to mail the chicken cross-pangaea, and then the whole-shelled
egg came sometime after. There was the asteroid and kids who looked
like mountains, and the bottle-necked shore so full of undiscovered fish
   we ate ourselves into a new species. Our mitochondria, beholdenly
glacial and ugly, already stuffed with laughlight hyacinth, gap-tooth
doorway dark, and hands book-pressed into leaves.
But it's the new world, and sisyphus is pushing and pushing and pushing
our love into a new body, over the equator of fleeting Middle American
spaghetti-strap tan, until it collapses down.
            We are nothing without the ocean. Our throats long for the days
                      when we read all the poetry together.
The earth honeyed with laughter, collectively I am nothing but sharp hip
bones, reused cells, and AndroGel. Half-asleep, you roll over and lift my
shirt and find nothing but snow. You are becoming a part of me.
The neighbors above us are cutting up the rug
          while the crosswalk pigeons siren pedestrians along outside.
We kiss, as is custom, and tell each other goodnight, but in a *See you
tomorrow* way. You turn back over, pull my arm across your body, and
say, *I don't want you to go. Not yet.*
              Darling, we lost our whole yard to city construction
                       and sold our bicycles for embryos.
How could I possibly leave you now, when wrong way signs look like
   lightning. When there are stars still pregnant with us, carrying our cosmic,
dumb little bodies to term.

MATT MITCHELL
after Molly Brodak

Has anything ever been more intimate
than becoming stretched out

around the guts of an ultrasound machine,
as if a body only knows how to fit

when a technician searches for signs of ovaries.

I am undone by all of what I haven't touched
in so long.

There is no light inside the parts of me
still shrinking.

They make airplane parts out of titanium hips
knocked loose from cremated bodies;

my doctor says I am at an increased risk
for strokes while on T,

just to maybe have a kid
who'll grow up to look like me.

How are we ever supposed to disappear gracefully
when there'll always be someone

who still recognizes the hole
in the sky that gets left behind.

The ultrasound technician presses
a jelly-enameled transducer

onto my pelvis and finds only my regret
for leaving my name in the mouths of so many men,

when every house I've gone into
is full of women,

and my body has plagiarized every last one of them.

PLUMS, WHICH IS JUST TO SAY

There's a scene in the *Evil Genius* documentary on Netflix
where Bill Rothstein calls the cops about a dead body hidden in his icebox.
But, as I'm watching this all play out,
as I'm washing my dinner of chicken nuggets down with a root beer,
all I can think about is that William Carlos Williams poem
about the plums in his icebox and his subsequent consumption of them.
Instead of immersing myself in the complicated plot
of the Erie Pizza Bomber bank heist,
I imagine Bill Rothstein on the phone with the Erie Police,
admitting to keeping a grandiose arrangement of plums in his icebox
instead of a dead body. I imagine this whole documentary based around plums
and nothing else. No dead bodies on ice. No conspiracies. No collar bombs.
Just frozen plums, the glow of my television trickling up into the moon's mouth,
and tomorrow, if tomorrow decides to come.
You come out of the bathroom in tears,
holding a plastic stick done over with pee and a +.
I have wasted my life. Whoops, wrong poem ending.

WHEN I THINK OF YOU A HABITAT

        Crying over you and your plaid shirt, camo shorts summer fit,
           just as I did when concessions stopped selling Pizza
      Combos in 2008.
Inside of you were two blue jays and a skylight. A beak careening glass,
a pin dropped and mistaken for a too-distant whisper.
    I have not seen you in a decade, yet I still think of you as if I have.
As if there is a chlorine pool in every backyard I fall into.
Why do I come back when everything here is a consequence,
like how Papaw and Donald flipped the Chevy at the bend
and Donald split his skull in half and then I was never allowed to bike
        down the road to Dan's house.
You were a flowering voice spoken into a landline phone,
a fragile wind snaking through the cowlick on my fat head.
I went so long not being held by anyone but the thought of you.
          I never finished leaving rings in the small of our backs
      to remind us how old we've become. I think you're 26 now,
but how can you be gone if I hear your laugh in every man's voice
        hollering down every city street. Ten years later and you look
right through me.
        Once, we didn't know the names of anything past tomorrow.
It was once just our hips shaking so delicately in the Mountaineer August
sun.
Who else am I supposed to be without you? What else could I ever be
        but a fruit stuffed in the split of bone you now call a jaw.

CLOUD TRAILS

Tell me how all of my high school crushes are getting married.
        How the woman I thought I once loved in 8th grade is about
        to have her first child.
If what Meat Loaf said is true, and we're damned if we get out and
damned if we don't,
        let me spend the rest of my life at the Trumbull County Fair.
Because I miss the big ride they rented from an amusement park in
Columbus.
One so big I cannot remember its name. An ex of mine rode it once.
She told me you could palm the moon once you reached the top.
    I suspect there is a big forgotten amusement park ride on every moon.
And summers are nothing but classmate weddings and half-baked
reunions now.
Remember when summers were fireworks in every inch of sky,
our own rain of comets. Museums of color kissing hollow air.
I watch fireworks and finally understand how every star I cannot touch
eventually dies.
There is hope alive here, there, everywhere. An offspring fuels the
generators in these peoples' hearts.
Whatever happened to sucking face by the chain-link fence protecting
the Apollo 11 replica downtown?
When we broke up with our homecoming dates in the McDonald's
parking lot.
Our mouths full of other mouths, teeth stained orange from
discontinued Hi-C.
It is true: I don't know what the word *heartbreak* sounds like coming
from a dying mouth, but I do know I have never been brave enough
to go on an amusement park ride.
I have never been brave enough to touch the stars.
Maybe I could have married them.

BACK WHEN WE HAD NOTHING EXCEPT OUR HANDS, WHICH GLOWED BEAUTIFULLY AND DREW PICTURES OF GODS DOING SOMERSAULTS WITH THE WIND, AS IF HORMONE IN THE FAT OF BONE LIKE MAKING A CASTLE OF AIR

Monday night, Johnny in the turntable saying *I am an old woman named after my mother*
as my hourglass body plumps into the shape of a bullet.
      The Flats dusk heavy, jarflies swarm the Huntington Bank ATM
across the street. Kids skateboarding down their front yard sidewalk,
they all remind me of the brother Mom and Dad couldn't conceive.
There's a hole in the sky where my body fell from,
and like a doorway I too am the hope before an empty room.
Airplanes and storks fly low above our apartment,
bird shit proudly sticks to every parking lot windshield but mine.
All the people we know are having babies. And so too are we.
Tuesday morning, you take us to get vaccinated near where they filmed
White Noise.
      When we come home, I lather testosterone onto a blade of shoulder.
Because what is an immune system response suppressant but an
avalanche soon curdled into the wind.
I have been living on cheated time long before we gave it a name.
      Is infertility hereditary? I don't know. Probably not. Maybe!
But the testosterone could make me stroke out at any moment.
      My whole heart could burst into smithereens from enanthate shock.
I truly am only a husband when the one-use needle gives me permission.
And to be a father, that would require eggs, sperm, an incubator,
and naive faith. When I say I love you, it is sometimes because we have
fallen into each other and are glowingly stuck like so. I used to say,
We will do whatever it takes, no matter the cost. You used to say,
Let's wait if we have to. Why rush into anything. Now we step outside,
unmasked.
I flash my tits at oncoming traffic. You dance yourself into a fart
and then we laugh.
Perhaps, together, we will create an army of intersex boys the shape
of space shuttles.

61

In a stolen sky, the clouds look like faces. The years blow by, and of course our cells still remember.

CYCLONE CAME AND WENT

When I was 6, I wanted to be a professional basketball player.
                I'm 25 now, and I still don't know how to be that.
I once fell in love with my art teacher, who had a tattoo of Honey Boo-
Boo's mom on his right thigh.
When someone drew a dick in permanent marker on the geometry
teacher's floor, the art teacher said *It wasn't Matt, or else that dick
would be much better drawn.*
God gave us hands like lifeboats and we wasted them. My mouth
is an enemy and my brain is even worse.
The sun is 32.2 billion in dog years. Imagine the shit it's done and lied about.
My therapist asks me to go on, so I say: In 3rd grade, I dug a moat
on the playground and called it God.
And then I cursed when someone tore it apart, banished to 10 days on
the wall for saying *fuck*.
I say: In 8th grade, I quit basketball because I shot jumpers from the
chest and ran laps for it.
I say: It is my gender that killed all the buffalo and apologized with nickels.
It is this thicket of mediocre road rage that destroyed Pangaea.
We also invented Coke Zero. How could you love any of this? Nobody
should.
                It's all incomplete, scrapped, and restarted.
There's a strip of Highway 30 in Iowa that looks like Ohio,
            with its farming malls and agricultural spaceships.
There's me and I'm reading Updike in my mother's car on our way west,
still thinking about games of smear the queer in backyards and on
lunchroom linoleum
10 years after the fact. Thinking of the ways we called each other *faggots*
but in a totally straight way
by the lunar module dedicated to Neil Armstrong,
      next to a McDonald's that never cleaned its soda fountains,
next to a Super K-Mart's corpse and a graveyard of butterflies.
Everybody is always giving us the benefit of the doubt,
even the highway of deer carcass stink and rumble strip DayQuil.
The son who murdered his mother on the county line and the man who
abandoned the golf course

now overgrown with ragweed and, lemongrass. We could've stopped them, couldn't we?
        And what about us at the party, leaning into each other by the
        fire pit,
                        saying we'll kiss boys someday.
How naive of us, to think we could just leave all of it behind and deserve to.
How bullshit of me, to take responsibility for a cock that wasn't mine.
        My therapist says I am missing the point, that we all
        just want to be loved and touched
by a sky unaware of all the ways we have been left undone.
        C'mon, she says, let's go see it. While we've still got some light.

A GENDER REVEAL PARTY STARTS A CALIFORNIA WILDFIRE AND, A WEEK LATER, THE SMOKE FINALLY REACHES THE FOOTHILLS OF NORTHEAST OHIO ON THE DAY WE GET TO SEE THE SONOGRAM OF OUR SON FOR THE FIRST TIME

after Orchid Cugini

It has come to my attention that middle school health classes forgot
   to mention how, for many of us, it will take countless mouths of smoke
just to make an offspring. The government agent trapped in my webcam
   must be sighing as I google *hormone therapy withdrawal symptoms
hereditary* for the umpteenth time in a waiting room, in-between
   systematic glances at the afternoon showing of Judge Judy, or the child
taking some crayola to the back wall, every so often.
I've been a labyrinth of wallpaper swatch and baby book anxiety
   since high school. Always hanging above me, a sequence of colors
soon-to-be in a nursery: blue and pink and then purple then yellow.
I am obsessed with the gyno's ultrasound monitor and its neutral
pixelated whiteness, if for nothing but the solitary hope of being in
   this moment forever, a singular chance at renting space in the
beforehand of certainty, not yet forced to accept the sureness of our baby
   boy's forthcoming sex-chromosomal coding that won't quite match up
with the other boys at his school.
Yes, I am quite nervous and scared about this. But I am also happy.
   So glowingly happy to put something on this earth before something I
can't control wipes me off of it.

TALKING TO MY SON BEYOND HIS MOTHER'S GUT JUST BEFORE THE BIRTH

I met your mother at a job interview I was told to bring a joke to. Is your refrigerator running? Wrong way signs looked like lightning when I watched her folding T-shirts over and over. The store was filled with a Spotify playlist touched by god or a Western Pennsylvanian, depending on how you squint.

Without lemon beer in a sweating glass at the bar across the way, there'd be no you. We sounded Hawaiian with our floral cooing; looked like skyscrapers with our necks peering over the tall tables. Weathermen pressed their pinkies against the wind looking for ice when we took to the sidewalk; the sun photosynthesized the downtown lunch rush just for us.

We talked about eloping to the tune of Elvis. I felt like I'd known and loved her forever. It was a Monday and the sky made itself into a gif. You kick the tummy wall like an ampersand curls. I once waved hello from the other side of the street and your mother smiled back an *I love you* before we started our shift, where we talked in paragraphs with our eyes from across the silent and freezing cold store.

VAMPIRE BURRITO

Of course I too was once a boy
with thin calves atop stacked bones

                                and someday you will become
                                something like that

but right now I am as much a he
as I am just trying to catch up

and you are so beautiful,
with your hands made of glass

                                and your blond headdress like
                                a thousand cowardly peacocks

moonwalking along the coastline
of a butter smooth forehead

in the nursery the moon landing
spills from the turntable

                                while I blow a raspberry onto your nose
                                like a sputter of bees in a Coke can

admittedly I didn't read the baby
books the library lent me

because yes you are mine
even in your manufacturedness

                    and yes of course I worry about you
                    every second of the day, but when your fist

                                  wrapped around my finger tightly
                                  I was too scared to hold you

or maybe I was just too scared
to hold the thought of you

        after all of those needled years,
          I still beg to be cracked open just right

                        beg to not look at you
                  and see someone else I loved once

do we ever really heal?
with you in my orbit I'd like to believe so,

                but most especially when you
           tumbled out of your mother and into my
           arms

like a decade. I saw the dracula
in your face endearingly and watched
the way the earth's axis suddenly fell
so glowingly into every part of you

MOTHER'S DAY

       The bodies on top of the bodies on top
            of the bodies are maybe not so much a feast
       but a wayward gloam of hope.
       In the waiting room I am surrounded by hope.
            In the examination room I am surrounded by hope.
       But too many people have lived through the grief of night
and wound up in a spotted paper thin gown
the next morning. Like Frank, I, too, have cut my nails
despite the improbability of there being a cure.
I should've called my aunt and wished her a Merry Christmas.
Should've donated to Wikipedia.
       I should've written more poems about eating pizza.
          Alas.
This house is full of sobbing; this house is full of felinas.
       The musk of the man in a lab coat who tells me
incurable and goes back home to his wife and kids
in a seven-figure home is particularly wet today.
       Once a month, it feels like a UTI. Sometimes a chainsaw.
There is a hem along my waist. Stretch marks,
       but possibly proof it wasn't always like this.
       I have seen enough Norman Rockwell paintings
       to feed a family of five. Hearts blink like a bright wound.
Freddie singing *I don't want to live alone* murmurs through the vents.
       The last great American whale was a starburst.
       A moon made of egg yolk and volleyball leather.
       I fear the mothership is here to take me home.
If that is true, I am ready to go. I have seen my ending
in the Rorschach of an ultrasound machine display.
Trim the windows, sparkle the cowhide in tea tree leaves.
Excavate the jelly out of my navel. Unhinge the clouds
            from the sky's jaw.
Full name. DOB. Current medications.
       How are you feeling today?
       This is my Barbara Streisand song!

The glissando of the EKG machine,
the warble of an X-ray being captured. Today, I am august.
       My insides flame in the color of a ripened womb.
Sentences shorten like breaths. A hand combs the cleft
       between my breasts. *More*, I think. I am starved
for touch, but only in a way that ends with a miracle.
On Ancestry.com, I am the 16th great-grandson
       of the king of a since-fallen empire.
My last name is now an open tab. Once it was a river
          where my folks' folks' folks' folks settled.
       This name hails from the town that created Mother's Day.
Everything looks good, I'll need to see you again in six months.
Some things make sense, even when most things shouldn't.

OLD BIRD

The dry score marks at the base of a Great Sequoia are not yet scars of dehydration, but welts of compression and struggle. Mausoleum of bark swallowing flames and pressure. Burn season's not yet here, but pretend you see anything other than a dying thing. Cancered at the roots, tufts of ash lived on Papaw's arms after he ignited his burn pile every month. The neighborhood smelled of melted plastic and brush smoke.

Mom likened his arms to tree stumps. He could lift an entire tractor up a few inches with his bare hands. Not long after the chemo, the skin on his biceps sagged into wings. He couldn't lift anything but methotrexate pills into his mouth. Close-proximity smoke inhalation was no longer just a typical Saturday.

A California botanist tells me a sequoia traps wildfire in its trunk and strangles heat until it becomes hieroglyphics in the name of the whole grove's survival. Like honky tonk summers swollen with sunlight stuck in a solar panel, great forests, and ancient trees, Papaw's arms will outlive all of us.

I hope we get together again, beside a lantern of wood-burning oven light. And he is retelling the story of a Grafton farmer who harvested eyeballs, for the 50th time. There he is carrying me to bed, like he always did. He swallows the last puffs of smoke slipping into the house from his backyard, as they head for my bedroom.

Groves of sequoias everywhere, they are rebuilding. So, too, am I, as I paint your nursery the color of Papaw's old Bel-Air and consider how I will begin to carry you.

THREE'S A CROWD

What thoughts I have for you this morning, my dear werewolf,
for I am now the same age as my mother when she met my father.
Nothing left for the hot summer jarflies to clean
but a tetanus shot and incurable suede.
Television infomercial of super sponge holler glow.
Bakelite seafoam plains mosquito-kissing the densed sky,
holed-out mountains spitting up licorice coal.
Our son is a pale one, all glue color body, blond locks, and plastic heart.
He drinks water straight from the spigot's mouth back home
and sleeps across the daytime. Soon he will have a purged accent.
Allergy test bedazzlings on back small.
His raised foot arches and clawing toes like mine.
Our baby burrito, beautiful and blued as moonlight.
Eczema arms and fruited wrists, be damned:
How I love him so, our son.
Cherry as the 10th song on the 4th Cat Stevens album;
his birth a Shakespearean one. Flowered and lassoed.
A crown of arthritis knuckles and uncracked backs
brought us into the light. I finger-comb his toddling hair
until he falls asleep on my shoulder.
Our kneecaps so ugly they could be chess pieces
and no one would think twice. They can't break us
if we remember we are skyscrapers.
Remember we are the best trucks in our class,
as voted on by JD Power and Associates.
Blondie, my Lost Boy, Nosferatu Jr., brittled fangs turned generational
recessive genes, and shotgun root of grandfather clock legs.
Together we're an army. We are the same and we sing beautifully.
Medical marvels when the world hasn't been so marvelous.

THE SHINING

Dropped the boy off at the sitter
                and went to a screening of *The Shining*
        at the Cedar Lee in the Heights.
It was an afternoon showing, a 3 o'clock getaway,
because matinees fuck and that's on god.
I got us Cokes: me a regular and you a diet,
                with popcorn and milk duds.
        We stuck our faces up close
to the neon of the coming soon posters.
We played the pre-movie trivia because it's tradition.
You didn't know any of the answers because it's tradition.
        The lights dimmed and the previews each said a prayer
        before saying goodnight to all six of us in the theater.
A movie theater sun looks good on you in the glow.
There was the opening shot, the shot we've seen a million times.
        The autumn leaves and the western vacancy of untouched land.
T H E S H I N I N G in Microsoft Word default font,
its powder blue serif body is forever nothing but water.
We giggled at the beauty of such a misleading introduction
        and started making out quietly, but brightly,
                because our bodies were so much more than water.
        They were ecosmart light bulbs wearing denim jackets,
        or two potato clocks dainty, pearled, and tonguing rainbow.
They say as soon as you set a clock it already starts going slow,
which must explain why we were making out.
Our meridian lips afraid of losing time,
        that guy four rows back yelled at us,
asking how we could possibly be making out during this.
And I said to him, *How could you not be making out during this?*

RECONSTRUCTION SITE

On our honeymoon, your mother and I worshiped Satan
by the pop cooler in a Pennsylvania Sheetz.
She became Princess Diana's 10th cousin by marriage,
so we held each other tight like oyster lips.
Temptation by New Order played through the ceiling speakers.
We paid for blue slushies and scratchers
with 2-dollar bills. I hid a Diet Coke for her
inside the lining of my jacket. Next to the nachos,
she asked me if I wanted to start trying.
I'd been writing a lot about having kids.
But what did I know about kids?
In other lives, I've died in ugly explosions of
3-out-of-5 reviews on Goodreads.
But in that moment, we were just a couple of nobodies
dancing on sticky checkerboard linoleum.
I said yes to your mother because I believed,
if we stepped just right, we would have,
right then and right there, become pearls.

HAPPY BIRTHDAY

Like crystals of calcium hardened
on the edges of a cheese block
in the forgotten bottom fridge drawer,
booger guts glue my morning eyes shut
and I comb out clumps of my grandfather's hairline
and not even the sun breaking through the window
wants to fall into me. The autoinjector pushes
too far into subcutaneous fat and out comes oxygen
and blood and then in goes a bruise.
After I clean up, I look in the hole
and see a terrarium of orchids slowly unpeeling.
I press a flashlight against my stomach
and watch the testosterone curdling inside.
Today is Tom Petty's *Southern Accents* birthday.
So many people in our galaxy, which is just one
of many galaxies in a universe still growing,
and Tom chose to have his album share a birthday
with only me, and that alone is worth celebrating.
I'll be 20-something according to my birth certificate,
but I am probably a MILF to someone.
The dog across the street weighs less than a dime;
like a doorway, I, too, was once hope before an empty room.
I go to work, spending the hours rearranging
now-playing marquees into your name,
in case you happen to drive by on your way home
from the Dairy Queen with an ice cream cake
tightly buckled into the passenger seat.
My hourglass body plumps into the shape of a bullet;
I step outside, unmasked, and flash my tits at oncoming traffic.
The sky above is stolen, all the clouds look like faces,
and Lake Erie is empty during lunchtime.
I go and meet a duck. I feed him hands of bread.
He's probably killed hundreds of men like me
in cold blood, but I am in a forgiving mood today.

DEAD BIRD

I always hated Aunt Carolyn's paintings of the house
        she and Papaw grew up in. I've always hated it
because she forgot to paint in the honeylocust
        that lived in their front yard, the way god's orange glow
            wrapped an entire mouth around a dusk.
        It's too late to live there, because the city of Grafton
        knocked it down a decade ago.
Everything is being taken away from me, slowly.
They say to love something you must first let go of it entirely.
        Dad, please explain how a painting can tell you everything
your dead father no longer can. Tell me about how the sunsets
        would swallow the house windows and turn them into lanterns
you could see from the satellites. How the lock on the front door
was jammed with smears of golden delicious apples.
        Honeylocusts can live an entire century, unless it's in a painting.
Let me tell you, the white clapboard siding speaks to me
        from the bottom of a Central West Virginia landfill,
where Papaw's handkerchiefs and Coors Banquet ghosts
live in collapsed lumber. Papaw moved to Northeast Ohio
to become a farmer. He wanted to be like John Wayne
in California. He ended up driving trucks for 30 years instead.
And once, while asleep in his cab bunk on the side of a Detroit highway,
he dreamt of his eldest son and awoke coughing up a shotgun.
        On his deathbed, he could see his old house,
its blue roof and clothing lines, the farmland stretching across a soil
where an ocean was stowed away beneath it.
        There's a sunset glimpsing beautifully through the
Honeylocust,
a spiring monument. My skin catches warmth from a bark
spoken of through toothless gums and a morphine accent.
        I am slowly becoming all of the places I've only driven past.

I WAS MADE TO LOVE YOU
after David Berman and Nick Drake

The baby never met the Neon Hollywood Cowboy
and maybe that is a good thing!
All he sees now are two bodies buried in chemicals
and oxygen, so full to the brim on hormones
they can be whatever they want to be!
Our love survived the insemination,
surely it can muscle him into a diaper.
I think we are good parents, because he laughs
like a hiccup and tells the cops to go fuck themselves.
For every day he smiles we plant a pawpaw tree
in the backyard. If we are lucky, our land
will soon smell like fruit. If we are lucky, the wind
will blow and his bones will not take shape elsewhere.
It's been more than a century of Thanksgivings
since my ancestors came to this land
and changed their names. What to show for it
but a bloodline prolonged by medicine?
I say that's okay as long as we've got whatever this is.
You and I are both old now but only in dog years.
The baby wants a snow globe so we give him a snow globe.
There is a cord between our hearts.
He is ours to spoil because he proved we weren't
spoiled ourselves. I am learning to love beyond myself,
and that is a scary thing. Not because his tiny laugh
might someday grow into a yell, but because the version
of me that made him came from a needle.
Mother's Day was invented in Grafton,
but what does the city have to say about fathers?
I am terrified that I am incapable of being gentle.
But he is our son, is he not? He is the salt
of my testosterone earth; the light of my beautiful life.
Because of him, the clamp has left my heart.
Someday he will watch you roll out of bed
and he will ask me if his mother has always been
so beautiful. And I will sing *of course* like

*The night she fell and the air was beautiful,
the night she fell all around.*
And when he awakes from a nightmare
in his crib and cries for us to save him, we will rush in
and say yes like *I am here and I am still here*.

AMERICAN WATER

The mermaids came just / after the A-bomb test in Nevada / Dad blamed Harding losing on the pharmaceutical dust / tornadoing around Mollenkopf Stadium / Mamaw sold my Lincoln Logs in the garage sale / and said kids haven't played with Lincoln Logs since 'Nam / I saw Joey down the road waiting for our bus / and he waved at me with a laser pointer he stole from the Scholastic Book Fair / we played hangman with our breaths / looking like handwriting stuck in January air / that spring, when The Melt came, all the lunch ladies / started microwaving the soybean burgers instead / I stuffed a million suns into the pockets of my cargo pants / and ate a Cry Baby Sour Ice cup all alone in my mother's classroom / like I was fucking Steven Glansberg / you were in an art class somewhere in another state / drawing pictures of all your beaches / the dealership said they put a moonroof in my Pontiac / so I could measure how far away god was / by ashing stars in the cupholder / and counting the mile-widths of toad-stranglers / yes we've seen thunder before / we just don't have a name for seeing it yet / can you believe we were all once ugly babies / hearing the This Charming Man riff for the first time / and thought, goodness, I hope the lead singer doesn't ruin this for all of us / or that we played hooky just to see what happened / to Rafe and his evil twin on *Days of Our Lives* / or that the Bush administration / took the last traffic light off the highway by my house / of course I miss / the suppers of buttered noodles and Coca-Cola / in front of a TV glowing *Man V. Food* reruns / turning the police scanner off just to hear How Deep Is Your Love / crawl out of Dad's living room stereo / and Dad saying Disco Demolition Night makes sense / in retrospect / or that one December when hometown garage band Acid / had their record go double-aluminum with no features / and there was snow falling in Manhattan on Christmas Eve / that looked like my mother in a hall of mirrors / back then our houses came from tin cylinders / with assembly required until the banks priced us out / and we couldn't afford an Uber / that would take us to the moon anymore / after the boys with Bill of Right forearm tats / stuffed toilet cleaner bombs into mailboxes / came the masculine street-fight lobotomies on SnapChat stories / I swear Chicken Fried blasting out of rusted Chevy S10s / will be the death of me / all of this and the stink from the falling steel plants / still disobeyed the wind and burnt down half the general store / all of this and the Ursuline cornerback still put a concussion / in Mario's head before Mario went and got drafted by the Giants / How romantic, the ways we've nuked each other to smithereens / just to come back pretty / the way the bar uptown closed every winter / and reopened under a new name / some say it was the hype / of the PlayStation 3 release that saved this city / for me, it was leaving and finding you

THERE'S A ROOM WHERE THE LIGHT WON'T FIND YOU
[WITH A NON-SEQUITUR ABOUT AN F4 TORNADO RIPPING THROUGH CHEAT MOUNTAIN, WEST VIRGINIA IN 1944]

My father and his father and his father all lived through a war,
                     but what have I lived through?
         Beneath the nebula of a throat where an Adam's apple once corked,
             there is an ecotone. A gateway in the shadow of doom.
Homesick for Hollywood, yada etc., as if any of it were ever mine to
begin with.
I am a pathological liar. The testosterone never worked,
         I just shook all the rocks out of my shoes
and a mirror then showed me the thin of a mustache
            and I declared myself well enough to parent.
What if, when I said I am only half a man without you,
I meant you. Not the Xyosted or the AndroGel or the placebo.
My hair is receding towards the clouds, but under the sand
of a forehead there you still are and there you are still glowing,
with a Chinese menu in your hand, excitable and sentimental.
         As if recession is progress, as if a cut of skin could be so pale,
like a birthmark sunbathing on a moon, as if and then again.
They put a needle in my testicles and pulled out a maybe.
Our combined latching had such little chance.
But then, a brand new baby boy arrived breached
and we raised him up to the heavens to get a good look, didn't we?
         Because a part of you and a part of me,
our modern miracle born sunny side up,
despite being scared to death of cracking his head like an egg.
Richard says there will be a niche in his chest where our hearts could fit
perfectly.
         Forever entwined by the inexplicable probability of us
         being soulmates even in fertilization,
the three of us will cut up the rug and hold hands while the walls come
tumbling down.

We'll watch him run to grab a sunset and be right there behind him.

[When Papaw watched a tornado send a 2x4 through the gut of a cow,
he then became propelled by the wind himself,
        as if straw pushing into the chest of a tree
        while 103 people died around him.
His daddy told him there's an ocean trapped beneath Appalachia.
So by the corn cellar, he and his siblings tapped their fists against the ground
like a knock. The smell of cold-packed meat sweat through the grass
    and they all thought it was water.
        To be tough as muscle then harvested for salt:
how could you possibly hold such a thing,

                                                           ]

CODA

I WANT YOU TO FEEL LIKE THIS CAN STILL BE YOUR HOME

It wasn't until I heard John Darnielle sing There's bound to be
a ghost in the back of your closet, no matter where you live,
that I understood what the Morgantown Boy meant
when he said just be cool at the Grafton Community Pool.
Full on coal and I love yous, soft as I imagine
the Marlboro Man's skin might feel like,
we traded cannonballs into the four-foot shallow end.
My aunt yelled God killed our beloved Matthew to my father,
as our coiled legs left pieces of us in the water.
The way I knew how to sketch tenderness after kissing
him like a sunset near the concession stand;
our mountain bodies full on Pizza Combos, our fingers smudging
the blip on the map where the Big Branch blew up in 2010;
hands hitchhiking through concaving indents between our breasts.
The way I looked for him every subsequent summer
and he never came back, I'm finding it hard to forgive.
I tended to a shelf of bibles at the end of a cul-de-sac; I prayed
to an Elvis PEZ dispenser; my stomach growled for Sisyphus
to push the boulder up through my throat and out of my mouth.
Maybe, in another universe, I give it all up just to want and be wanted.

FLEETWOOD MAC FILMS THE HOLD ME MUSIC VIDEO ALONE IN THE MOJAVE DESERT, 1982

Of course it was a hot Northeast Ohio summer when Papaw taught me how to fry steak-umms in a skillet without crusting the sides. It was a decade before he died in a hospice bed from lung cancer, as the beat of Independence Day lights rattled the house. When Fleetwood Mac, dressed like archeologists, dust off the casket of a piano from beneath golden Mojave sand, I am reminded of 100-degree heat lapping against a body. Because there was Stevie Nicks in a red dress, her nose full of coke bloat, an emaciated stomach beneath. Her pale skin like clouds, as if our skyful gazes upwards could unstrap themselves from a horizon we were fooled into thinking we owned.

While in the presence of beauty, even the English language feels unworthy of definition. Because when I say the entire band felt so sick while filming a dedication to the only good part of *Mirage*, I mean they eventually got their shit together within an inch of fatal dehydration. When I say Stevie stumbled across the desert in platform heels, I mean she was about to let herself uncoil at the touch of a loving hand tensed beneath a shoulder. As if my papaw, too, told her, *Don't be afraid*, when approaching the rising heat, as he was ready to show off a perfect spatula flip.

Dirty oil spit up against hovering arms, but a cord formed between our hearts. We let the steak-umms cook so long they burned, so we watched NASCAR instead and went hungry. But when he was dying, and a gurgling ocean of morphine and stomach acid ate away at him, he couldn't speak, because his dentures were in a cup of alka seltzer on the bathroom sink, his vocals in the basement of his throat. If I'm being honest, Fleetwood Mac filming the Hold Me music video has nothing to do with any of this, other than we all once learned what it meant to survive on an empty stomach, if for nothing but the sake of spending time with someone we loved for just a few moments longer.

A CABIN IN UTAH

I consider one day an apocalypse. Not a McCarthy apocalypse, but a you and me apocalypse. End times where we have a cabin atop a hill on abandoned Salt Lake farmland. The cabin, we go sore making it ours. There are cannibals next door. They watch us hold our test tube son in the air and zip him around the yard like a rocket ship. On weekends, I travel north to find mountains for our backyard. I paint pictures of you on our porch, sunset backlit and all, amber hair bending blue with 7 o'clock stars and all. I turn wheat stalks from meadow earth into neckline jewelry for you; buried treasure spoons into rings. Every day, the cannibals come by the house with their mouth knives and stink. They ask kindly if they can have us for dinner, but we give them cheese from our goats in exchange for another day. *Be careful how many times you eat your way through a sky*, you say to me each time. *You could end up a cannibal in someone else's story*. I learn to catch rainbow trout but never actually do. I just play Yahtzee with you after supper. When we run out of score sheets and the dice yellow, we trace numbers in the air with sparklers. We make the numbers up on the spot. I draw each day by hand. The kiddo likes listening to Johnny on the crank record player. *Shoot the moon right between the eyes*, he sings at us all day. He digs up the backyard looking for D.B. Cooper's money. We know someday he'll ask what Appalachia was like, and someday we'll tell him: *Picture us dancing together in a heavy rain and then you'll know*. The cowboys sound like New Yorkers, the New Yorkers sound like gone, and the gone sounds like air. There'll be nothing in sight to break for miles except the mornings and our hearts, if our apocalypse leaves us any. It's all sky and ground and me and you. It's always been me and you, under our blanket fort made out of forever. When our boy jets off to college, maybe then we will, finally, become birds. And if the mountains ever question their kidnapping, we'll give them cheese from our goats in exchange for another day. Pinky swear.

Poems in *Vampire Burrito* originally appeared, in various forms, in *Poetry Online, petrichor, The Boiler, blush lit, Southeast Review, HAD, Salt Hill Journal, Black Warrior Review, drDOCTOR, DearPoetry, Cosmonauts Avenue, The Spectacle, perhappened, Tinderbox Journal, Mutiny! Magazine, No Contact, Sporklet, Cotton Xenomorph, Ours Poetica, Protean Magazine, Half Mystic,* and *Rejection Letters.*

Some poems from this book appeared in my chapbook, *Grown Ocean*, published by Word West in September 2021.

They say you thank everyone under the sun in the acknowledgment section of your first book. Where do we go from there? I must say thank you, first and foremost, to Kevin Latimer and Brendan Joyce for giving this book to the world. To the intersex community for teaching me new ways to love myself and the roads I take. To my family, to my friends. To the people who've come down from their moons to offer feedback on one of these poems. To every editor who's published work from this book. To my fellow nervous wrecks and hormone monsters. To you, reader, for opening the front cover and taking a chance on the story I decided to tell. Thank you, endlessly, from the bottom of my sappy, healing heart.

This book is dedicated to all of the vampire burritos, wherever they are at this very moment. I hope you're dancing and I hope the rain has settled.

NOTES

"Vampire of the North Coast" contains a line from "Real Estate" by Richard Siken

"Gray and Gold" contains lines from "Poem ['Lana Turner has collapsed!']" by Frank O'Hara and "Scheherazade" by Richard Siken

"There's a Room Where the Light Won't Find You" is titled after a lyric in "Everybody Wants to Rule the World" by Tears For Fears

"State Bird" contains a line from Allen Ginsberg's "Howl"

"White Noise" contains a lyric from "Hello It's Me" by Todd Rundgren

"Building a Bird" contains an allusion to "I Remember, I Remember" by Mary Ruefle

"City of Light, City of Magic" is titled after a lyric in "Burn On" by Randy Newman

"We Had an Apartment in the City" is titled after a lyric in "Hello in There" by John Prine

"Chinatown" contains a line from *Chinatown*

"iPhone Notes" contains a lyric from "Radio Ga Ga" by Queen

"The Day of the Expanding Man in Reverse" is titled after a lyric in "Deacon Blues" by Steely Dan

"Nuclear Saturdays" contains an allusion to a lyric from "Thrasher" by Neil Young and Crazy Horse

"Neil Young Gave That Speech From the Moon" is titled after a quote in *The Saints of Newark*

"Half of Me is Ocean, Half of Me is Sky" is titled after a lyric in "Walls (No. 3)" by Tom Petty and the Heartbreakers and contains quotes from *Six Feet Under*, "Thick as a Brick" by Jethro Tull, and *My Girl*

"Operator [That's Not the Way It Feels]" is titled after the song of the same name by Jim Croce

"Pretty in Pink" contains an allusion to a lyric from "If You Leave" by Orchestral Maneuvers in the Dark

"John Carpenter's *Halloween*, 1978" contains a lyric from "Streets of Philadelphia" by Bruce Springsteen

"I Was Breathless Upon Every Mountain Just to Look For Your Light" is titled after a lyric from "Concorde" by Black Country, New Road

"Plums, Which is Just to Say" contains allusions to "This Is Just To Say" by William Carlos Williams and "Lying in a Hammock at William Duffy's Farm in Pine Island, Minnesota" by James Wright

"Cloud Trails" contains a lyric from "Bat Out of Hell" by Meat Loaf

"Back When We Had Nothing Except Our Hands, Which Glowed Beautifully and Drew Pictures of Gods Doing

Somersaults With the Wind, As if Hormone in the Fat of Bone Like Making a Castle of Air" contains lyrics from "Angel From Montgomery" by John Prine

"Mother's Day" contains a lyric from "I Want to Break Free" by Queen

"Reconstruction Site" is titled after the song of the same name by the Weakerthans

"I Was Made to Love You" is titled after a lyric in "Concorde" by Black Country, New Road and contains lines from "Serenade for a Wealthy Widow" by David Berman and "From the Morning" by Nick Drake

"American Water" is titled after the album of the same name by Silver Jews

"There's a Room Where the Light Won't Find You" is titled after and contains lyrics from "Everybody Wants to Rule the World" by Tears For Fears, contains a lyric from "Werewolves of London" by Warren Zevon, and contains a line from "Road Music" by Richard Siken

"I Want You to Feel Like This Can Still Be Your Home" is titled after a quote in *Stranger Things*

"A Cabin in Utah" is titled after a lyric in "Sign on the Window" by Bob Dylan and contains a lyric from "Clocks and Spoons" by John Prine

MATT MITCHELL is an assistant music editor for Paste, and a poet, essayist, and culture critic from Northeast Ohio. Vampire Burrito is his second book of poetry.

www.ingramcontent.com/pod-product-compliance
Lightning Source LLC
Chambersburg PA
CBHW061730070526
44583CB00024B/3082